THE PEOPLE ALONG THE SAND

THE PEOPLE ALONG THE SAND

Three Stories,
Six Poems,
and
a
Memoir

Anthony Brandt

Introduction by Bill Henderson

CANIO'S EDITIONS

This book is for
Evan,
who has the most understanding heart
of anyone I have ever known

Canio's Editions
P.O. Box 1962
Sag Harbor, NY 11963

516-725-4926

Table of Contents

Introduction

by Bill Henderson

They don't make them like Tony Brandt any-more—tall, thoughtful, silent. So silent, in fact, that I almost never got to know him. For years we sat side by side at Sag Harbor's American Hotel bar and I never heard the guy speak.

Luckily for the both of us, I tend to enjoy an extra glass of schnapps now and again and I turned to silent Brandt one day and demanded that he justify himself. The more we talked that afternoon, the more I realized the guy not only could speak but I agreed about what he spoke of. He even looked like me. We were brothers. And have remained so for almost ten years now.

Since you will never guess it from reading these pieces, I will tell you another thing: Tony has an amazing radio voice. Talk about authority! When Brandt hit the local air waves recently for a political party and said, "Sag Harbor voters, you must know this..." the entire town listened up. The fellow could play radio God and I would believe him.

What else? He's a terrific cook—actually has enough confidence in his machismo that he wears an apron in the kitchen. He's collected a superior library of rare books; he's authored *Reality Police,* a book about the mental health profession that was so incisive it got him sued (he won); he has knocked out more pieces of fascinating journalism than I could list here; he essayed a column for *Esquire* magazine a while back—the most popular feature in the magazine; and, he is one of the most important essays editors on the cosmos—for the annual Pushcart Prize.

In short, this guy is a guy to be reckoned with. Ask his wife Lorraine. She's been reckoning with him for over ten years now and she adores the guy—even if they are married.

Now about this reader. Brandt's written voice is as authoritative as his radio voice—he wastes no words and doesn't spare himself, particularly in the memoir of his divorce. I have seldom read such a wrenching self-examination. The stories and poems address a variety of situations and subjects. Here is an author who does not stick to safe and pat subjects. And always there is the sea, just at the edge of his imagination.

If you like the sea, you will love the Brandtian vision. If you don't love the sea, there is little hope for you anyway. As Brandt knows, the sea is everywhere. He helps us see this, and hear it.

Tony Brandt is a sea captain you can trust.

Preface

An architect friend of mine describes the beach as not so much a place as the transcendence of place, a border between two realities, and another friend calls the people attracted to it, who feel they must live next to it or very close to it, edge people. Count me in. When the chance came to move to Sag Harbor, six-and-a-half miles from the beach, I did not hesitate. I spent my summers as a child at the Jersey shore and I always knew I would come back to the beach at some point in my life, live near the water, close to the edge of my native continent, turning my back on it, as it were. In order, I told myself, to see it better.

I have been here now more than ten years but I still feel like a summer guest. It is hard to feel rooted living near the edge; it is hard to believe that the place itself is stable, that it will last. How old is Long Island? A mere 15,000 years or so? In Sag Harbor the soil is half sand; it runs down the street where I live after every rain. Recently a storm took forty feet from the dunes in sections of Bridgehampton and twenty-five houses in Westhampton Beach. When I was a child a hurricane deposited a thirty-five-foot power boat in our front yard in Brant Beach, New Jersey. You do not forget these things. The edge shifts. This is a frontier of a kind, and it is not stable. If global

iii

warming continues and sea levels continue to rise, large sections of Sag Harbor may be under water in a hundred years or so.

Perhaps this subtle sense of instability and contingency, this uneasiness about the land, if you will, is why the beach and its environs have no literature. The English Midlands have *Middlemarch*, contemporary New York has *Bonfire of the Vanities*; the Mississippi, *The Adventures of Huckleberry Finn*. Willa Cather immortalized the prairies. There is no end to sea stories. But even Walt Whitman, who was born here, hasn't much to say about Long Island. And the beach itself? I can think of nothing but Matthew Arnold's "Dover Beach" and Robert Frost's "Neither Out Far nor in Deep," from which I take my title, and two poems hardly constitute a literature. Literature needs, I believe, to be rooted somewhere; it needs a sense of place, a sense that people, even if they are moving through it, stand in some relationship to the landscape. And the beach is not a landscape but a horizon. It is where you go to escape the land, as my architect friend says to transcend it. As Frost says,

> The people along the sand
> All turn and look one way.
> They turn their back on the land.
> They look at the sea all day.

Which brings me to this modest little book, which is all about men and women, that is to say about love and its failures, set entirely on or near the beach. It is my attempt to make a contribution to our feeling for this highly provisional habitation, where it is so hard to feel wholly at home, this almost spiritual metaphor for the temporary and contingent character of existence. And what is more contemporary and contingent than love? One might say that all of life, to extend the metaphor, is a summer romance.

Think of this as beach reading, then, a little book about men and women and the difficulty of making love last anywhere, but perhaps especially here, where the sun can be pitiless and the horizon stretches out like a map in all directions and the surrounding ocean, vast and restless, is the very image of mutability.

THE PEOPLE ALONG THE SAND

Three Stories,
Six Poems,
and
a
Memoir

Skimmer

"Did you see his neck? " Parker yelled over the noise of the outboard motor.

"What'd you say? His neck?"

"Yeah, the back." Parker pointed with his free hand to the back of his own neck. "Shoe leather," he shouted. "Lined and cracked. Looked like dried mud."

"Well, they don't call them leathernecks for nothing," Jerry shouted back.

"You think he was in the Marines?"

"I didn't mean that." Jerry shook his head. "Maybe. I don't know." He shrugged. "But that's got to be where the word comes from. In the sun all the time. Skin exposed all the time." Jerry was sitting in the bow of the boat; he had to twist around to shout back at Parker, who sat in the rear, steering. "Probably spent his whole life on the docks. Back of his hands, too." Jerry pointed to the back of his left hand with his right. "I saw them."

Parker nodded. "Under the clothes," he yelled toward Jerry, "they're all white. I've seen these old guys before. Never take their shirts off. Never go swimming, never go to the beach. Live here all their lives, never learn to swim."

"You serious?"

"Yeah. Really."

It was going to be hot, that was obvious. The air had a whitish haze to it, there was no breeze, the surface of the water lay as flat and calm as sheet steel. Parker pointed the little boat west southwest toward the mainland, visible as a line of marsh, then a line of trees, in the distance. To the south, over open water, they could see the towers of Atlantic City floating above the white ribbon of reflected heat that rode just above the horizon. The city itself was over the edge; only the towers were visible, uprooted, impossibly suspended in the air.

It was a little more than half an hour to the fishing grounds around Long Point.

"I used to sail around here," Parker yelled.

"What'd you say?" Jerry twisted around to look at him.

"Used to sail around here. Little boat called a Duster. Plywood boat."

Jerry nodded, then turned back toward the bow. He was wearing khaki shorts and a white T-shirt that read "Epcot Center" on the front. The T-shirt annoyed Parker. He hated clothing with signs printed on it. Why make yourself into a walking advertisement? Parker himself was wearing an old long-sleeved dress shirt, to protect his arms from the sun, a pair of khakis, tennis shoes. He wore a hat, too, against the glare, a khaki fishing hat with a long green plastic brim that he had found in the closet that morning. There was already, even this early in the morning, a certain amount of glare; it was a kind of quality added to the light, an intensification. Even under his hat Parker was squinting.

Ahead he could see the boats gathering in the deeper water off Long Point. They passed a small marsh island, Parker giving it room to starboard. The whole bay was shallow except where the channels ran and at places like Long Point, where the tidal currents were strong. Parker peered over the side. He hadn't noticed whether it was low tide, but it must be, he decided. He could see the eel grass, as thick as a field of wheat, undulating below.

"You could walk across this bay," he shouted at Jerry.

"What?" Jerry shouted back, turning around.

"I said you could walk across," Parker repeated, pointing over the side.

Jerry nodded. "Yeah. Shallow."

Parker fell silent after that, staring over Jerry's shoulder toward the boats at Long Point, increasingly distinguishable through the haze. They passed another marsh island, this one slightly larger, slightly more built up in the center than the last. Parker wondered idly whether they would survive global warming, the rising sea level that went with it. He looked to the left of Long Point toward the long nameless marsh that stretched out into Beach Haven Inlet from Tuckerton, on the mainland, and the other marshes this side of it, big sprawling green pancakes, all mud, greenhead flies, sharp spiky marsh grass, huge mussel beds. He hated marshes, and loved them. He remembered poling his own rowboat along the edge of the marshes near the house when he was a kid. At high tide the edge was just under water; there was a lip to it, an overhang, and the blueshell crabs hid under it and if you were real slow you could pole in there and drift along and ease your net underneath the crabs and then in one quick jerk you had them. Had them for dinner, dropped in boiling water still alive. It was cruel, he supposed. But they were crabs; they didn't even have a brain.

The marsh smell, too: rich, rotten. He knew about marsh gas. All that decay. The greenheads loved it, bred in it. He had been swimming once, his mouth open just above the surface of the water, and a greenhead had flown right into his mouth. The memory could still make him shudder. Greenheads were vicious biters, but they were slow. You could almost always kill them with your hand.

Parker turned his gaze to the fish factory on the other side of the long marsh. Somebody had told him once that they processed menhaden there, turned it into fertilizer. He thought menhaden was a kind of herring, but he wasn't sure. There was nothing like fish for fertilizer, he knew that. The factory stood alone, its only neighbor the abandoned Coast Guard station a mile to the east. The fish factory had always interested Parker. You could see it from the waters three miles to the north, near where Parker had grown up, while you couldn't see Atlantic City in those days as the buildings weren't that tall. Parker had always thought it had a kind of romantic feel to it. Anything standing alone in some vast waste place had to have a romantic feel to it.

"Hey, Jerry," he yelled over the intense buzz of the Evinrude.

Jerry turned around.

"We could go there later if there's no fish." He pointed toward the fish factory. Jerry turned and looked.

"What is it?" he yelled back.

"It's a fertilizer factory. Menhaden."

Jerry looked at him, puzzled, for a moment. Then he shrugged and turned away.

#

"How far is the horizon? Do you know?"

"Seventeen miles," Jerry answered. "Or maybe it's eleven. One of those two numbers."

"I used to know," Parker said.

Parker was bottom fishing, using squid for bait. He had never made up his mind whether he really liked to fish, but his father had done it, and at least it got him out on the water. It was his father's equipment, in fact: his old rod, his tackle box with the slowly rusting hooks, the stiff catgut leaders, the lead sinkers. The equipment had fallen to Parker when his father died. He sometimes thought he should bring it up to date, but it was easier not to. Parker preferred to keep the whole thing simple. Rent a rowboat once or twice a summer. Go out for a few hours. Even a rusty hook could catch a fish. He handled them carefully, though. He knew that rust equaled tetanus if you cut yourself with it. He should get new hooks. It was plain inertia that stopped him. If he had to go to all that trouble, he might wind up not going fishing at all.

Sailing, he supposed, was what he really wanted to do. But to own a sailboat, with only three weeks vacation—how much could you use it? Still, he would have preferred to go sailing. Sailing had always refreshed Parker. It gave you, he told himself, room to maneuver. What was the German word? Lebensraum. Room to live. To breathe. But sailing was one thing, a sailboat something else. A sailboat was just another kind of trouble. It had to be maintained, it had to be stored in the winter, painted in the spring. You had to scrape the bottom periodically. It wasn't worth it.

"So Jerry, how's your family? How's Peggy? You haven't said a word about her."

"No, they're okay," Jerry said. Jerry was casting and reeling in, casting and reeling in, working the middle depth hoping for weakfish. "Peggy's good. She's looking for work; the bank cut back, you know. You don't know of anything, do you?"

"Where, in the city?" Parker asked.

"Anywhere, really. I mean, within reason. We don't want to move to Maine or anything like that."

"I'll ask around. But things are not good where I am, either."

"Yeah?"

"Yeah, we've had some losses. All the insurance companies are in trouble. It's not underwriting, it's poor investments. Everybody thought the big ride was never going to end. Can you believe how stupid these people are? I mean these guys, these top guys, they've got company cars, big houses, perks up the ass, but can they think? Can they think?" Parker was getting angry; this was a subject that could easily make him angry. "You know, they put all this money in office buildings and malls and shit and the projections were right in front of them. It wasn't going to happen. You know that; you've got your own agency. There aren't enough people to fill all that fucking space. They live in a goddamn fantasy world."

"Yeah, I know what you mean," Jerry said. "That's why I went into business for myself."

"So how are you doing?"

"Wait a minute," Jerry said. "I think I've got something." Jerry's line was tugging in the water. He jerked his rod toward him, then reeled in. "Shit," he said. "A blowfish."

"You caught a blowfish?" Parker asked, looking over the side toward Jerry's line.

"A blowfish."

"You can eat the backs, you know," Parker said. "Chicken of the sea. But you need a lot of them to make a meal."

"I know," Jerry answered him. He had pulled the blowfish into the boat and was twisting the hook out of its mouth. "But I promised Peggy weakfish. A big three-pound weakfish. That's what you said was out here." Jerry tossed the fish back into the water. "Maybe I should try the bottom. Or a bigger hook."

"Well," said Parker, "the bottom hasn't done me a hell of a lot of good. All I'm getting are crabs eating my bait."

He didn't think of it until later that Jerry hadn't answered his question about how he was doing. He decided not to press the issue. It was great to own your own business, but it had to be the right business. A real estate agency was not what you wanted to be in at this particular moment in time.

#

"So if you could do something else with your life," Parker said, "what would it be?"

"Something else?" Jerry had taken off his T-shirt and was rubbing sunblock on his shoulders. "Why would I want to do something else?"

"I don't know. Don't you ever think about it?"

"Not really."

"Yeah? I do. Every time I come out here I see those towers down there"—Parker pointed to the south, toward Atlantic City—"and I think, I should have been a gambler."

Jerry stared at him. "A gambler?"

"Don't laugh," Parker said, stiffening.

"I'm not laughing." Carefully, Jerry stifled a smile.

"I mean, it's what I do now, you know. All day long I underwrite insurance policies. You think that's not gambling? It's just not my money I'm gambling with."

"But man, that's a big difference when it's not your money."

"I'm not arguing with you. But that's what I'd like to know. You know what I mean? I'd like to know if I've got the balls for it."

"Did you ever do it?" Jerry asked.

"Do it? What do you mean?"

"Do it. You must have been to Atlantic City. Did you ever gamble at all?"

"Penny ante stuff. Slot machines. Twenty dollars worth of quarters. Sheila wouldn't let me do any more than that."

"Yeah, well, she's got an investment to protect."

"But if I wasn't married, you know, I could do it. I could gamble. You ever see *The Cincinnati Kid*? Steve McQueen movie?"

Jerry shook his head no.

"It's all about poker. It turned me on, let me tell you. Because I did that once. I got involved in a game, it went on for five straight hours. Not high stakes or anything. But I was down maybe forty dollars, and I came back, I walked away something like twenty-seven dollars ahead. It felt terrific."

"But as a way of life," Jerry said. "Those guys don't lead stable lives."

"So what's so wonderful," Parker replied, "about a stable life?"

"Marriage, my friend," Jerry answered promptly. "Marriage, kids. A house you can call your own."

"So to speak," Parker cut in. "What the bank doesn't own is what you mean." Jerry stared back at him again. "Look," Parker went on, "this is stupid. We're not catching anything here but blowfish and crabs. Why don't we take the boat over to the fish factory."

"Yeah, okay," Jerry said. "But what's there? I can see it, but what is it?"

"I don't know. I've been coming down here all my life and nobody ever called it anything but the fish factory. I think they make fertilizer. But that's the point. I've never taken the trouble to go see the fucking place."

"Yeah, all right," Jerry said. "We might as well go."

#

It took Parker longer than he had anticipated to find his way through the marshes. He tried Middle Channel first; it was the first one he came to. But the channel turned due south, away from the fish factory, almost as soon as he got into it; and then the cedar branches sticking out of the bay that marked the channel ran out in what looked like open water. But it wasn't open water. Parker peered over the side and could see that it was shallow, so shallow that at full ebb tide it looked like the marsh would emerge. As it was the propeller was already stirring up mud.

"We've got to go back," he yelled at Jerry.

"What?"

"We've got to try another way," Parker yelled up to Jerry again. "This is the channel to nowhere."

"Yeah, okay," Jerry yelled back.

Parker turned the boat around and re-emerged into Little Egg Harbor and turned west toward the main body of the marshes. In the distance he could see buoys, and what looked like a wider channel, although it was difficult to tell at a distance, the lines of marsh blending into each other. But the presence of the buoys meant that there had to be a route; and there was. He saw another boat disappear into it.

Once again the channel turned south, away from the fish factory, but Parker was following the main body of the marsh now, the great clenched fist of green that jutted out from Tuckerton toward Little Egg Inlet and the North Atlantic. It was built up enough, and the channel was low enough, that they could no longer see the fish factory across it. They caught occasional glimpses of the road, a bridge over a creek, and once in a while they saw a car. Egrets stood at the edge of the waterway, one leg tucked up under them. Jerry had put his shirt back on; the green flies were out, not a lot, but it was best not to leave skin unnecessarily unprotected. Neither of them tried to talk. When they reached Big Sheepshead Creek Jerry yelled back at Parker, "You going in here?"

"I don't know," Parker replied, slowing the boat. "What do you think?"

"No channel markers," Jerry said.

"Yeah." Ahead of them lay Little Egg Inlet, the blue-green waters of the ocean; in the distance they could see surf breaking on sandbars.

The creek turned abruptly northwest, back the way they had come, then due west at right angles. It was dangerously shallow.

"Jesus," Parker said, "I hope we don't get stuck in here."

"Keep going," Jerry yelled at him from up front.

Neither man said anything then for the half-hour it took to navigate through the creek. A great blue heron took off when they got near, circled behind them and alit again in the creek waters. They watched it take off, its long neck folded back on itself like a piece of rope. At two-fifteen in the afternoon they came out suddenly into Great Bay, less than a mile from the fish factory.

"There it is!" Parker yelled, idling the motor.

"Yeah, I see it," Jerry said.

Directly behind to the southwest, eleven miles further, lay the towers of Atlantic City, trembling in the haze above the vast and impenetrable reaches of the Brigantine Marshes. Parker pointed toward the line of green that marked their demarcation.

"That whole area," he said, "is a sanctuary."

"A sanctuary?"

"Birds," Parker said.

Jerry turned around and looked at him. "So aren't we going to the fish factory?" he asked.

"Yeah. I was just looking at all this. I've never come this far before."

But Jerry was staring now at something toward the west. "What the hell is that?" he asked.

"What? What are you looking at?" Parker said, turning around in his seat. Then he saw it in the distance, moving just above the surface of the water, its wingtips almost touching it at every beat, flying along the edge of the great marsh directly toward them.

"Jesus," Parker breathed.

"What is it?" Jerry said.

"It's a skimmer," Parker answered.

"A skimmer?"

The bird came on, its white underside perhaps two or three inches above the surface, the wings two feet across, maybe more, its head at an angle that allowed the lower beak to break the surface of the water as it flew, a beak like a large pair of scissors, or maybe a compass. The wings, they could see, were black like a crow's above, but the bird was all white underneath. It came on fast, passing within ten feet of the boat; then it wheeled gracefully up and off toward the southwest and disappeared over Seven Island Marsh toward Atlantic City.

"That was kind of amazing," Jerry said.

"I haven't seen a skimmer since I was a kid," said Parker. "Not in twenty years, anyway." He looked toward where the bird had disappeared from view. In the distance the hot sun glinted off something metallic on the roof of one of the towers. He turned and looked at Jerry. "I thought maybe they had died out," he said. "Become extinct, you know what I mean?"

"Yeah," Jerry replied. "But did you notice, it wasn't even afraid? It flew right by us like we weren't even here. I almost felt I could have reached out and touched the wing."

Bauhaus

It was late Friday afternoon when John turned the gray Mercedes into the long level driveway. The off-white walls of the house had taken on a yellowish tinge in the fading light. "All the windows are on the ocean side," he said. "From here it looks kind of monolithic."

Linda sat forward in the passenger seat, her right hand on the dashboard, staring at the house. "Oh?" she replied absently. Then she said, "It's not at all what I expected."

"What did you expect?" John asked.

She settled back in the seat. "Well, I guess I thought you'd have a more traditional house. Shingle-style, or something like that. You know," she went on, "like one of those houses in Maine."

"Sorry to disappoint you," he said drily.

"Oh, I don't mean that I don't like it," Linda said, turning to him and putting her hand on his arm. "I'm just surprised, that's all. You know how you build up an image in your mind, and then you see the real thing...."

"Well," he said, steering the big car into a small rectangular parking area near the steps that led up to the front door, "this is the Hamptons. It's not like Maine. You get a real mix of architecture here."

"Yes, I know," she said, "It's just that I expected you to have something more traditional."

John turned off the motor but made no move to get out of the car. "The truth is," he said, "Janet picked the house out, not me. Not that I objected or anything. I don't think I knew what I wanted. But you don't like it."

"No, no," she said, "it's not that. It's very impressive. Who designed it, do you know?"

"I used to know," he said. "I mean, I know it's International Style, or Modern. I think the guy's name begins with a B."

"Ward Bennett?" she asked.

"I don't know. That could be it. Janet knew; she knew all about it. But do you like it?"

"John, really, it's very impressive," she said. "So many modern houses—they're melodramatic; the architects want to make a statement, and the house is all about their egos. But this is very clean, very simple." Linda was staring at the house as she spoke. The entrance wing, facing northwest at an angle from the rest of the house, did indeed show no glass; it was all concrete, a severe mass of wall broken by the outline of a wide concrete chimney. Low, wide steps rose to a set of tall, heavy wooden doors that were heavily carved and looked vaguely Spanish in style.

"So you think I got my money's worth for it? I paid a lot. I mean, one hell of a lot of money."

"Oh, no doubt about that," she replied. She was still looking at the house.

"Well, come on," he said, opening the door of the car. "Let's get in out of the cold."

#

Linda was tall and thin with a great mane of curly black hair and she wore clothes so well that almost anything looked good on her, but she made dinner for him in a pair of old slacks and a bulky sweater that almost completely disguised her lines. They ate in the big kitchen at the square metal-and-glass breakfast table. The late winter sun had long since set and she had filled the room with candlelight. It gave the matte black Calphalon pots hanging over the island countertop an uncharacteristically rich glow.

"So you can cook, too," John said, leaning back in his chair.

"Is there cognac?" Linda replied, getting up and starting to clear the table. "Would you like some cognac?"

"Next you'll be offering me a cigar," he said. "The cognac is out in the dining area in the liquor cabinet. I'll get it. The snifters are in that cupboard over there, behind the other glasses."

She was putting the dirty dishes in the dishwasher. "Are you going to keep the house?" she called after him as he disappeared into the dining area. He came back in a moment, carrying a half-empty bottle of Hennessy by the neck. She brought two snifters over to the table and sat down.

"Keep the house?" he said, pouring the cognac. "Is that what you said? Am I going to keep the house?"

"Yes," she replied, taking one of the glasses in her hand. "Are you going to keep the house?"

He looked at her quizzically. "Why would I want to get rid of the house?" he asked. "You really don't like it at all, do you?"

"I just wondered," she said, swirling the cognac in her glass. She waited a moment, then went on, glancing sideways at him. "You told me that Janet picked it out; I thought maybe you'd want to get rid of it."

"So I can move to Maine, right?" His tone had turned dry again.

"Come on, John, don't be offended. I do like the house. The house is perfect, in fact. But I have trouble seeing you in it. After all that wood paneling in your office, and the leather chairs...."

"That's just traditional WASP lawyer stuff, Linda; you ought to know that," he said.

"But it suits you, don't you think?" she asked.

"I don't know. I always just took it for granted," he replied. "You grow up into it; my father had furniture like that in his office. I think the clients like it. It's very solid, very reassuring. You don't really choose it as a personal style. It fits the profession. The solidity of the law, that sort of thing."

"Well, I'll admit that I haven't known you very long," Linda said. "But this really just seems like cognitive dissonance, if you know what I mean. I mean, you are sort of old-fashioned and traditional, aren't you?" She paused, leaning back and looking at him reflectively, her hands holding the cognac cradled between her breasts. "In the best sense," she went on. "Honest. Upright. Given to smoking pipes."

"You know I don't smoke," he said quietly.

"I know," she said, the tone of her voice softening. "But if you did smoke, I bet it would be a pipe. It wouldn't be cigarettes and it wouldn't be cigars."

"You're probably right," he conceded. "Although I'm not sure it wouldn't simply be part of the image. The old WASP law firm." He smiled ruefully, looking at his glass. "But what a fate: to be nothing more than an image."

Linda reached over and touched his hand. "I wouldn't be here, John, if I thought that's all you were."

"Well, what kind of person do you think I am?"

She pulled back into her chair. Then she spoke with an air almost of deliberation. "I think you're old-fashioned and a little stiff and a little off-putting. But that's just the outside. Inside I think you're very very gentle, and very very smart, too. And considerate. Kind. You're a sweet, wonderful guy. And there's not a lot of those around."

He looked away from her, embarrassed. "It's hard—"

"That's why I don't think the house is right for you," she interrupted. "I mean, I don't want to make a big issue of it, but it just seems cold. Perfect. Too perfect. And you're not that cold. Not at all."

"I just seem that way," John responded, the dryness back in his voice.

Linda bounced out of her chair. "Come on," she said, "let's forget the whole thing. Let's go make a fire. Let's have more cognac. I've had a hard week, a nasty week. The photography business is hell, John, you have no idea. Deadlines, pressure, competition. I need a shoulder to lean on." She reached out her hand to pull him up. He let her lead him away into the living room.

#

They were walking on the beach, half a mile or so from the house and within sight of one of the freshwater ponds that lie just behind the beach here and there in the Hamptons. The day was clear, the wind light but chilly from behind them.

"You seem a little remote today," John remarked.

"Do I?" she said, glancing toward him. "Sorry." Then as an afterthought she added, "But look who's talking."

"Well, with me it's habitual. That's my style. A little off-putting— isn't that what you said?"

"I did say that, didn't I." It was not a question but a statement. "And I'll have to pay for it, won't I."

"Oh," said John, smiling at her, "it won't cost you much. A few kisses, maybe."

"I guess I should have dressed a little more warmly. It's cold out here."

"Do you want to go back?" he asked.

"No, no, I'll be all right. It's too beautiful. I don't want to leave." She wrapped her arms tight around her body.

"We could—"

"No, really. I'll be fine."

22

They walked in silence for a while, keeping to the hard-packed sand close to the water's edge. Winter storms had lowered the level of the beach and narrowed it, but up on the dry sand where the tide could not reach them remnants of summer debris could still be seen here and there: a flip-flop, a battered boat cushion, a soda can that someone had flattened and then left behind.

"What are you thinking about?" he broke in finally.

She didn't answer immediately. "Well, to tell you the truth, I was thinking about your furniture." She waited a beat, but he did not respond. "No," she went on, "that's not quite true. I was thinking about Janet. I was wondering what kind of woman would like furniture like that. Want a house like that. That style." She turned to look at him. "What was she like? I should say, what is she like? Is she spare and severe like the house?"

"Do you want the abandoned husband's view, or the objective outsider's?"

"You decide. I'll read between the lines."

"Well, she's smart, I suppose."

"What kind of smart?" asked Linda. "Street smart? Book smart?"

"Street smart...." John thought for a moment. "I don't think anybody from her background gets to be street smart. She lived a very protected life. School in Switzerland, that sort of thing. Her family had a great deal of money. No, what I mean is that she knew a lot. She was clever about things. The house is a perfect example. It's all her doing. I didn't interfere at all."

"It's odd that you should wind up with it, then," Linda remarked.

"Well—I don't know. She used to tell me she was doing it for me."

"For you?" Linda looked over at him in surprise.

"Yes. She'd say, 'You like things to be perfect, John. Well, this is going to be perfect.'"

"Perfect. That's the word I used," Linda said. She stared out at the ocean. "Well, it is perfect. I bet all that furniture is original."

"It could be. It sure as hell cost a lot."

"You can tell from the age of the leather. You can tell just by looking at it. She went to a lot of trouble."

"Well, she was that way. Very meticulous. She read up on things. As I say, she was smart."

"But was she like that?" Linda wanted to know. "It's such a severe style. People with money usually go for chintz and old English furniture. For antiques." Linda stooped down and picked up a white pebble struck through with mustard-yellow veins. "I mean, is she a severe person? Cool and businesslike? That's what I think of when I see that kind of design. Form follows function, the lack of decoration..."

"Well, no. Not really. She had class." He frowned, thinking. "It's a little hard to be objective, you know. She did leave me. But I have to be honest. She had real class. She just...."

Linda waited for a moment. "She just what, John?"

"She just wasn't really happy with me, I guess. Sometimes I think the house was her gift to me. She knew she was going to leave, so she picked out this house for me. I think that's what she meant."

"That makes you cool and businesslike," Linda said. "What about her?"

"I can't really say she was cool and businesslike. She was really quite a warm person. She's very thin, you understand. Can a thin person be warm?" He seemed to be thinking out loud. "You're thin, and you're warm." He put his arm around her, pulling her toward him. "Maybe not right now, though."

"Was she passionate?" No sooner had she framed the words than she stopped and pulled away from him. "No, I'm sorry," she said. "I withdraw the question. It's just that I don't understand the house. I don't understand a woman liking anything so—so abstract, that's the word. Clean and abstract. Uncluttered. Cerebral. There aren't even any family photographs around. The place looks like the architect just walked out the door."

They had passed the pond and they lapsed again into silence. Small, crisp waves rolled in from the Atlantic. Linda stopped to pick up another pebble, looked at it absently, then dropped it. She made no move to start walking again. John stopped a few steps further on and looked back at her.

"What's wrong?" he asked.

"I'm getting cold," she said. "I think I'd like to go back."

"Okay," he replied.

They walked back the way they had come, Linda buttoning her coat to the chin against the wind, which was now in their faces, and burying her hands deep in her pockets.

It was John who finally broke the lengthening silence. "I think it's true. I think she did the house that way for my benefit. I'm not sure she liked it all that much herself."

#

The Barcelona chairs, four of them, faced each other across a large low Noguchi coffee table. John had made a fire and Linda was curled up on the chair nearest the fire, staring at it. She turned her head, the great mane of hair spreading out on the top of the chair behind her, and looked over at John, who sat catty-corner across the coffee table, a Scotch, straight up, cradled in his hands.

"Have you ever noticed," she said, "that Barcelona chairs are always set up like this, facing each other? I mean, you never see them just kind of scattered around a room."

He didn't answer for a moment. Then he said, "You really do hate this place, don't you."

"No, really, John, have you ever noticed that? I mean, they're great, classic chairs, but they really demand this kind of arrangement." She turned back toward the fire. "The idea of order in East Hampton," she added.

"The idea of order," John repeated. "I like order."

"I can see that."

"Well, don't you?" he asked, challenge in his voice.

"I love order," she said emphatically. "You've seen my apartment. You know how neat I keep everything."

John didn't reply.

"And if I had had money...," she said, not finishing the sentence.

"Yes?" John said expectantly.

"I don't know," she said. "I guess I'm too— what should I say?— eclectic a person to go in for something like this. A place like this, where the style is so uniform..." Her voice trailed off. "It seems sort of—I don't know. Impenetrable."

"Meaning that I'm impenetrable," John said, a trace of resentment in his voice.

"Or maybe," she said, ignoring his last remark, "maybe spare is the best word. Spare. Ascetic. Zen. The best word for this place, I mean. You could meditate in this place. Very easily. You don't meditate, do you, John?"

"No," he replied, "I don't meditate."

She hesitated before she spoke again. "Look, I don't want to hurt your feelings. I know you love the house."

John leaned forward and put his drink down on the table. "I never said that I loved it," he said stiffly. "I happen to like it. I'm comfortable in it, that's all. And I respect it."

"I know you do."

"And it's clear to me that you don't."

"I'm sorry, John. I'm being stupid." She looked away, out through the long glass wall toward the ocean, the foam of the breaking waves in the faded afternoon light looking like streaks of pale pink crayon across the slate gray water. "It's very unfair of me to make these kinds of judgments, isn't it?" she said. She glanced at him. "The house just took me by surprise, I guess."

"You think the house reflects me, don't you?" John said, still a little angry. "Even though Janet did the whole thing."

She reached her hand across the table toward him. "John, don't you remember? I said you were sweet and gentle and old-fashioned. I think you're all those kinds of things."

"That was yesterday," he said. "Yesterday you thought I liked wood paneling, too."

#

Linda was soaking in the bathtub when he walked in. She had placed candles on the sink and the top of the toilet, and the light from them glistened on the wet skin of her shoulders and breasts. The mirror was dim with steam.

"I'm sorry," he said. "I'll go down the hall."

"John?" she called out. He had closed the door behind him as he left. Now he stood just on the other side, his hand still on the knob.

"Yes?" he said.

"What are we going to do?" she said.

"What do you mean?" he replied.

"Well, I was thinking," she said. "Maybe we should go back early."

John stood still, waiting for her to say something else. Then he said, "It's the damned house, isn't it?"

"It's not the house, John. Really, the house is perfect just the way it is."

She didn't immediately say anything more. John waited a moment longer, then turned away and walked off down the hall.

The Scarf

Sammy left his house around nine and walked west toward Madison, then up Madison to Jermain and over to the cemetery. It was a walk he took once or twice a year, a kind of pilgrimage, he supposed, though a short one—five or six blocks, maybe half a mile. He wasn't sure, didn't care. He was slightly hung over, which, he told himself, he certainly didn't need to be on a day like today. It was late June. A cold front had come through the evening before and the air was crisp, the wind fresh out of the north. He almost needed a jacket. A good sailing day, if the wind held. He would get coffee and an egg sandwich from the deli on Main Street, then think about it. But first he wanted to visit the cemetery.

It was laid out in a grid, like a tiny city: city of the dead. He wondered if that was what they had in mind. So American, he thought, to lay everything out in a grid. Sammy was Australian by birth, but he had been educated in England and thought of himself as English. He followed the same route he always followed, up the leftmost aisle, past the gravestone that read "The End is Nothing / The Road is All"—it was a source of wonder to him that anybody could carve such a stupid cliché in stone—then past Corwins and Conklins and the Edwards clan, Hayworths and McClellans, Reeves, more Conklins, toward the broken mast monument commemorating those

who had died in the whale fishery in the nine-
teenth century, the Ahabs of this place. It was
handsome and tall, solid white limestone, the
mast broken and leaning over, a rope curled
around it, and under that a square block carved
with names, and on one side a low relief of men
in small boats harpooning whales. Nearby were
the graves of the old sea captain and his wives.
Sammy felt, although he couldn't explain why,
that it was a fitting juxtaposition. Two kinds of
hero, perhaps. The old captain fascinated him.
Five wives, and he outlived them all. You could
still read the inscription on one of the wives'
graves.

> Behold, ye mortals, passing by
> How thick the partners of one husband lie,
> Vast and unsearchable the ways of God,
> Just and severe his chastising rod.

Sammy himself had shed two wives, but of course
it wasn't the same. The old man didn't divorce
them, he outlived them. All five of them. He wore
them out. "Behold." What a powerful word, he
thought. He couldn't help but wonder what the
old man thought about it all. He must have
thought God was punishing him. Or maybe not.
He didn't stop marrying, did he?

Sammy looked around the place a few more
minutes, then headed for Suffolk Street, which
was narrow and close-set with houses and a pleas-
anter way to walk downtown. Main Street was
already crowded when he got there, people lining
up for breakfast in the Paradise, buying papers at
the Ideal. He noticed Geoff Rigsby emerging from
the Ideal, the *New York Times* tucked under his
arm. Sammy would have preferred to avoid him
but it was too late.

"Good morning," he said.

"How are you, Geoff?" Sammy replied.

"Good, good. And you?"

"Hung over." Sammy moved past him toward the deli. "Got to get some coffee into me before it's fatal. See you."

"Sure," said Geoff.

Like two dogs sniffing each other, Sammy thought. He bought his breakfast and walked on toward the wharf, where he ate sitting on a piling staring at the harbor. With coffee in him it didn't seem quite as cool as it had. The hangover seemed to be fading, too. Normally he held his liquor well. He tried to remember how many drinks: three? four? The bar had been crowded and it hadn't been that easy to get drinks. Then he remembered that someone had bought him a drink. And he had paid for a round. He took another sip of coffee. The sins of the evening shall be visited upon the morning. Even unto the tenth generation, is that what it says? His thoughts returned to the old captain, privateer, whaleman, and husband five times over. When the last one died, wouldn't he have felt a sense of triumph? To have outlived them all? Isn't that what you would feel? He put his coffee down and rubbed his temples with both hands. Of course the divorces had just felt like failures. Abject failures. But then, to outlive people is a victory, isn't it? A kind of victory?

#

Geoff sat in an old, faded canvas chair on the deck behind his house reading the travel section of the *Times*. On a small table beside him stood a mug of coffee, partly consumed, and a pile of orange sections on a glass plate. His wife, Alice, in an identical chair, sat opposite reading the book reviews. The sun was warm, and the house protected them from the wind.

"I ran into Sammy Gilbert in town," Geoff said.

"Oh?" Alice replied, not looking up.

"He said he was hung over."

"Nothing new about that," Alice said.

They were both silent for a few minutes, absorbed in the paper. Then Geoff spoke up again. "I was thinking we could maybe ask him over for dinner some time."

Alice glanced at him over the book review. "Now that's a switch," she said. "I thought you couldn't stand him."

Geoff folded up the travel section and put it down beside his chair. "I never said I couldn't stand him. I said I couldn't stand the type."

"You mean the type I once had a relationship with." Alice's face was half hidden by the book review; Geoff couldn't tell whether she was smiling at him or not.

"I mean compulsive womanizers."

"Like Sammy," Alice said.

"All right, all right," Geoff said, irritated now. "Let's not ask him to dinner."

34

"I'm sorry, sweetheart," Alice said, lowering the paper and smiling at him. "I didn't mean to tease you. If you want to ask him to dinner, that's fine."

"He seems like a decent guy," Geoff said. "He's in the business. I think maybe I've been silly.... You know."

Her smile gathered a tenderness into it; it was a smile that always made him melt a little. "Yes, I know," she said.

"It's not like he ever did anything to me," he said.

Alice didn't answer him this time.

"I'm friendly with Stewart," Geoff went on, "and he went out with you."

"That's right," Alice replied. He didn't say anything more and she went back to the newspaper. Geoff leaned over and picked up the theater section; he read the paper in the same order every week, first travel, then theater, then the front page and the Long Island section and the magazine, then the book review. He never read the sports section. He watched baseball games on television from time to time, but he didn't want to read about them. Baseball relaxed him: so much strategy, so little action. The game was almost intellectual, like chess. It surprised him that it was so popular in such an anti-intellectual country as his own.

The lead story in the theater section was on David Mamet. He liked Mamet's work, but he couldn't get into the piece. He glanced at Alice from time to time; she had drawn one leg up under her, and her blond hair, which she refused to cut to fit the season's fashion, was spilling over her shoulders and half over her face. Like Veronica Lake, he thought. Alice was almost as beautiful; her eyes were a little too closely set together, but she was a stunning woman, no doubt about that. He often wondered why she had married him. His line was that she could have had anybody, but she had picked him.

Indeed she had had plenty of men, he knew that. She had been married once before, to a banker. It had lasted three years, with no children. When she found out she couldn't have children, he left her. Her standard comment, delivered with a little crooked grin, was that he was a male chauvinist prig; he had dynastic visions, she would say, and wanted to be another Rockefeller & Sons. Then came years of fooling around, of affairs. Then Geoff. Who had never been married, although he had lived with someone for five years. Who was three years younger than Alice, and not nearly as experienced. Safe harbor, he had concluded. Alice was looking finally for a port in the storm of her sex life, and he was it. He didn't like to think about it. It made him bitter. Yes, she had picked him. He knew he should take it as a compliment. She was gorgeous. She loved him. She told him she loved him. He had no reason to doubt her. But he suspected she was just tired of it all. She wanted a stable relationship, and there was nobody around more stable, more trustworthy—more unexciting, he always added—than himself.

"So let's set a date," Geoff said.

"A date?" Alice looked up at him.

"To have Sammy over. With some other people."

Alice put the book review down in her lap. "You're serious about this, aren't you?" she said. It was more a statement than a question.

"Yes, I am," Sammy replied. "It's time to get over this—the silliness. The jealousy."

Alice looked at him blankly, giving nothing away.

"Two weeks?" he asked. "Right after the Fourth?"

"It's your party, Geoff," she said. "You do the inviting."

#

It was indeed a good day for sailing. The wind was brisk without being so strong that Sammy couldn't handle the boat himself. The only drawback was the spray the wind slapped into the cockpit when he was cutting through the waves on a tack. A Flying Scot was a nice little day sailer and it was easy to maintain, but Sammy had dreamed for years of something bigger and better, one of those long, sleek racing boats all in wood, an IOD, maybe, or even better an old E-sloop. It would have been like having an antique Jaguar. Not that anything like that would have kept out the spray. But with something sleeker, at least you'd have looks to go with the discomfort. Still, on his salary, he didn't have much choice.

He was out of the harbor before he thought about where to go. He hesitated to sail west, between North Haven and Shelter Island; if he got stuck in Peconic Bay with the tide against him it would take all day to get back. It was one of the disadvantages of sailing a small boat in these waters; the tides were unusually strong. Best, he decided, to sail out beyond Cedar Point. He could always get back in with the wind behind him, no matter what the tides. In the meantime he could have brunch in Greenport. When he came to Buoy No. 1, then, he turned east, off the tack onto a reach up the channel. Reaches were fun, a wild ride across the wind, not into it. The Scot may not have been pretty but it was fast. He liked the speed, loved it. He hadn't put the jib up; that would have been too much to handle. Even without the jib, though, the boat moved well in this wind. He caught himself smiling; then he thought, oh, what the fuck, and whooped out loud. Hangover's gone, man! Fly, baby, fly!

The exhilaration lingered as he rounded the southern tip of Shelter Island and started to tack up toward the lighthouse at Cedar Point. He should have brought gloves; the sheet was already beginning to rub his hands sore. But he didn't really mind. He looked around; Northwest Harbor always surprised him with its size; it was like a great pregnant belly. A kettle of water. Whaling ships had sailed through here. He had always wondered how they had done it, how they maneuvered big ships like that down the zigzag channel that led into the harbor to Long Wharf. Under sail—they had no power then. The old captain would have known, of course. He would have known those waters by heart: every rock, every swirl of current. Like the contours of his wives' bodies. Rocks emerging like breasts swelling out of their clothes. The tide was high, the rocks were covered now. But they were there. Sammy knew they were there. Knowing exactly where was the secret.

Up ahead he could see a cormorant floating on the water, its body mostly awash so that only its long neck and its head were clear of the waves. He steered for it; laboriously it took off ahead of him, curving east and then south toward the sand cliffs of Barcelona. The Cedar Point Lighthouse, long disused, stood outlined against the low profile of the North Fork in the middle distance. Around Cedar Point to the east lay Three Mile Harbor, then Gardiner's Island. A day sailer definitely limits your range, he reminded himself. He had never been as far as Gardiner's Island. It would be fun to take a girl there, he thought. With a picnic. Sammy regarded sailing as a test for the girls he took out. If they liked it, he knew he was going to like them. He no longer had much use for hothouse types. Those days were over. There was too little adventure in life as it was.

#

"Alice?"

"I'm upstairs, Geoff," she shouted down to him.

Geoff hated to shout; if people wanted to talk to each other, he felt, they should go find each other. He trotted upstairs and found Alice in the bedroom changing into her running shorts.

"I'm going for a walk," he said. "I take it you don't want to come."

"I think I'm going to do the circuit," she said, pulling on a pair of Nikes. Geoff knew the circuit; it was a three-mile run out Noyac Road to Stoney Hill, then up Stoney Hill to Brickiln, then back down to the village.

"All right," he said; "see you later." Geoff retreated to the living room to look for his favorite cap, which had a blue Agway emblem above the brim. He liked wearing a cap over his thinning dark hair; he was tall, hats looked good on him. He needed a hat to balance his nose, which was long, thin, and slightly hooked, like a Roman nose. A source of bemusement for Geoff; there was no trace of Italian blood anywhere in the family's past.

It was not an aimless walk. Geoff had a route in mind: up Main Street to Palmer Terrace, out Palmer Terrace to Jermain, then left on Jermain, down Suffolk Street, then east toward Sammy's house. It wasn't the shortest way but that was beside the point. The day was perfect for walking, and this was the route with some of the best old houses. Geoff loved old houses; he knew all the styles: Federal, Greek Revival, Queen Anne, Carpenter Gothic, and many of the combinations. Palmer Terrace had a magnificent old Queen Anne with a tower, a sun porch, another porch above that, and three shingle patterns. It was a house whose layout he couldn't predict from the outside; he would have liked to have knocked on the door, asked to see it, but he never did. Very Freudian of himself, he had decided, to be curious about the insides of houses. But you had to know that the Queen Anne would be complicated inside. Like his wife, he thought. All too much like his wife. He liked Federal-style houses as well, with their classic balanced layouts, the central hall, two or sometimes three rooms on each side. There was a terrific example on Main Street, but someone had ruined it: closed up the front door and made it into a bay window, Italianated it. Was Italianate a word? He didn't think so. Still, it fit. Main Street was a marvel generally; it was a virtual museum of domestic architecture. All the types were there, even a brick town house that looked like it belonged in Philadelphia. You had to wonder about the builders: did they know what they were doing? Did they consciously create all this variety? He didn't know. Probably no one knew. Maybe over the years it just happened by itself.

At the end of Palmer Terrace he turned left past the cemetery to Suffolk. It was on Suffolk, he remembered, that one of the houses had *faux bois* walls in the center hallway, plaster painted to look like pine. He had seen the house on a house tour and the pine had struck him as strange. Why pine, when mahogany or walnut would have seemed so much richer? The owner told him he had found the faux bois under five layers of wallpaper. People were incomprehensible; who would cover up such a wall? Failures of taste always disturbed Geoff.

The lots were small on Suffolk Street, the houses large; the total impression was of a kind of density, of mass. He noticed for the first time that the porch on one house had a copper roof: very rare, he knew. He was looking forward now to seeing what Sammy's house looked like inside. Assuming he invited him in. Sammy had never made an effort with Geoff, but Geoff figured that was his fault. He could probably read Geoff's uneasiness; it must have been written all over him. Time to get over that. The man had slept with his wife, but for Christ's sake it was before Geoff knew her. Well, he knew her; everybody knew her. But he'd never dated her, not until later. Why, she had asked him at a party once, haven't you ever asked me out?

He hadn't known what to say. Then he had blurted out the truth: beautiful women frighten me, he had said.

I don't bite, she had said.

Even so it had taken him weeks to screw up his courage and call her. It was indeed true, beautiful women did intimidate him. He didn't know why; he had seen lots of average-looking guys with gorgeous women. Sammy was average. Sammy was no hunk. It was the accent, that was it. The accent, and the English charm. Australian, he corrected himself. Some men just had the confidence, the assurance. He knew he didn't. Why did she marry him? The perennial question.

What was he going to say? He would face that when Sammy opened the door. Be polite. Keep his thoughts down. Him inside her, her mouth sucking him off. Not something he should be dwelling on right now. It was hard. He had to get over this; he had had relationships, he had slept with other women for Christ's sake, not a lot but enough. Enough. Done those things with them. Five years with Marian. It was time to grow up. He was nearly forty. Everybody had a past. That's what Alice always told him: if you're over seventeen, Geoff, you've got a past.

#

Shortly after noon, when Sammy was well beyond Cedar Point, halfway to Greenport, the wind died. Within fifteen minutes it was nearly calm. Sammy knew what would probably happen next. When it picked up again, it would have shifted out of the southwest. That meant he would be tacking back the whole way. It was going to take twice as long to get back as he had expected.

He raised the jib, but it didn't make much difference. He decided against Greenport. Everything would take too long—getting there, eating. Probably the best thing to do would be to come about, try to run a little with whatever wind there was. Variable light breezes, that's how they would describe this on the weather report. Yeah, he thought, like a woman. His mind flicked to yesterday, the moment she had said no. Mixed messages. Yes I want it no I don't. Please Sammy, don't. Fickleness thy name is woman. That wasn't the line, of course. Might as well be. He would send her the scarf in the mail. No. Let her come and get it.

Gardiner's Island stood five or six miles to the east. If the wind had held he might have risked it, he thought. It would have meant going without lunch. It looked like he was going to do that anyway. He should have thought of it, should have brought something, a sandwich from the deli, a few cans of beer. The water had that effect you get in light breezes, areas of ripples here and there, other areas that were flat and shiny like mica. The ripples didn't mean anything, didn't mean the wind was coming up. They only meant it was "variable." Sammy had been sitting on the deck; now he sat down in the cockpit. There was nothing he could do about it. You can't control the wind. Maybe, he thought, he should finally get an outboard, attach it to the boat. He had been a purist about sailing too long: no motors. Really, why not? he asked himself. The wind dies in these waters all the time. All the time.

#

"Sammy?"

Geoff had knocked and waited, knocked and waited. When there was no answer he had triedthe door and, finding it open, poked his head in and called. He called again.

"Sammy? It's Geoff Rigsby. Are you here?"

The house had that kind of intense quiet to it that you only notice when you're listening for footsteps or some other sign of movement. Geoff wondered whether he should go in. He didn't really know Sammy. Maybe he was out getting the newspaper. No, he'd seen him downtown on his way to the deli. That was at least an hour ago. Two hours, maybe. If he went in and Sammy came back, how would he explain it? Embarrassing. It was embarrassing enough just to be there. But he could leave a note, couldn't he? Just pop in, find a piece of paper and a pencil, tuck the note into the handle of the door. A perfectly innocent gesture, wasn't it?

From what he could see from the door there was plenty of note paper around. Piles of manuscripts littered the floor of the living room. He could see a table against the far wall that must have functioned as a desk; it, too, was covered with manuscripts. But otherwise the place was orderly; there were no half-empty beer bottles sitting around, no clothes thrown over chairs. Nice to see that in a bachelor's house. And the room was charming. There was a small fireplace against one wall, with a simple, even primitive mantel. Small windows, twelve on twelve. Probably much of the glass was original. Looked it, anyway. It was an old seaman's cottage, like so many houses here. The white plaster walls looked old; you could see where they bowed out, how the house had settled. A little beauty, this house. Steep stairs went up from behind the door. To the back, through a doorway, Geoff could make out the corner of a dining room table. The kitchen was probably behind the dining room. Saltbox construction.

Geoff decided to risk going in.

#

The wind did come up again, from the southwest, as he had predicted, and sooner than he had hoped; he had known calms last most of the afternoon. He tacked back the way he had come, through the gap at Cedar Point. It was ten or fifteen minutes before he noticed that he wasn't making any progress. He was in the same position in relation to a clump of three scrub oak trees on the long spine of Mashomack that he had been when he last tacked. And in the same position, on the opposite tack, to Cedar Point Light.

"Damn!" he said. "The fucking tide is going out!"

He looked over the side, checking the current. The tide was going out all right, and the wind wasn't strong enough to drive him through the gap against it. He was sailing, he was even heeling a little, but he was going nowhere.

"Shit!" Sammy kicked the well of the centerboard. "Now what do I do?"

He looked around. There were no other boats in sight. Now, he thought, is when he needed power. But no—Sammy the purist can't have power. Stupid Sammy. He was getting hungry, and the idea of waiting for the tide to turn didn't thrill him. He considered his options. A tow from a passing power boat—but there were none in sight, only a couple of sailboats in the belly of Northwest Harbor, another out towards Gardiner's Island. Or he could walk the boat back along Mashomack. Sail over, get out, wade along the edge of the beach and tow the boat behind him with the mooring line. Sammy the Volga boatman. The water would be cold, of course. But it was better than sitting out there hungry. What the hell, he thought. Life's a beach.

Sammy brought the Scot about and headed straight for Mashomack. He couldn't run it onto the beach; the bottom was rocky, he might have damaged the hull. About ten feet off shore Sammy brought the boat into the wind, lowered the sails and jumped out. He was in water halfway up his thighs, and it was cold, no doubt about that, but bearable. Moving up to the bow, he took the bow line and slung it over his shoulders and started walking. He grinned a little to himself. He had wanted adventure in his life, and here it was. So to speak. A woman would have gotten hysterical, of course. "I'm so hungry, Sammy, why didn't you remember to bring some food?" Not many pass the test, do they? he asked himself. Always talking about maturity, telling me I'm immature because I play around, don't want children. Alice couldn't have children—probably should have married Alice. Not that she isn't better off with that wimpy Geoff. Now *he's* mature, right? Maturity is that whole Freudian canard. Well, damn Freud. He didn't believe in Freud, and that's what you had to do: believe in him. Don't believe in marriage, either. What's mature about marriage? It's a trap. Ask the old captain—he survived them all. Of course in those days you had to get married to get any.

A Cigarette, long, sleek and gaudy, powered through the gap at top speed; when the wake hit him the waves got him wet above the waist. He could see the people on the boat looking at him impassively. He suppressed the impulse to yell at them. What good would it do? They wouldn't hear him over all that noise. He just had to get through it. Another fifty yards, maybe a hundred, the main force of the tide would be behind him. If the wind held he'd be home in an hour.

#

Geoff didn't notice the scarf at first; it was laid over the arm rest of the couch so neatly that it almost seemed to belong there. Then he saw it and mechanically, as if his arm were not under his control, reached over and picked it up. Silk, a

Deco design of some sort. He felt a fine sweat break out on his forehead as the thought swept over him: was it Alice's? Was this hers?

He stood there staring at it, trying to think. She had so many scarves, so many clothes. He held it to his nose. The smell was familiar, but he couldn't be sure. He knew her perfume: Poison. Little black bottle. But was this it? It was like wine; you had to have a nose for it. He could sense the panic rising in him and he tried to stave it off. She had gone out the day before. Shopping, she had said. Came back with nothing. Had she been wearing a scarf? He tried to remember, tried to visualize her; he had looked up at her when she went out the door waving to him, but it was all so mechanical. After a while, everything gets mechanical. Hellos and good-byes, see you laters, gestures of all kinds. Blue slacks? Brown? He remembered that she was wearing slacks, but he couldn't remember the color.

Was there anything around her neck?

He couldn't remember.

There would be signs. If somebody's having an affair, there are always signs. She would make love differently. You'd catch her in small lies. The phone would ring, and whoever it was would hang up when you answered. Geoff wandered into the dining room, then back into the living room, still holding the scarf. He couldn't remember any signs. Nothing was happening, he told himself. This is just me, this is my crazy imagination, this is paranoia. It could be anybody's scarf.

A really clever woman, though: she'd know how to make sure there weren't any signs.

He knew he should leave but he felt rooted, nailed down. For a moment he considered searching the house, looking for other pieces of clothing. The bedroom, maybe. No. He was being crazy, nothing was going on, nothing. He stood staring at the scarf, gray and pink, the colors soft, pastelly, the edges hard. It could be anybody's scarf, anybody's. Sammy is a known womanizer; it could be anybody's.

Alice was more than clever, Alice was unknowable. And she wore scarves sometimes. He just couldn't remember; he hadn't noticed what she was wearing. Even if it was hers, maybe she'd just come by to talk. It didn't have to mean anything. She'd known Sammy for a long time. Longer than him. He was so jealous, she might have just not told him. She said she loved him. She does, doesn't she? An image kept intruding into his thoughts; he tried to put it out of his head, to hold it off. You're being stupid, Geoff. This is you being stupid, Geoff, this is not reality. But he could see it; it was strong, familiar, Alice in bed, the sheets thrown off, her long hair spread out on the pillow and damp with sweat, and Sammy, yes it was Sammy on top of her, he was pumping into her, she had her legs up and around him, her heels were digging into his buttocks, driving him deeper, spurring him on.

Geoff stood there staring at the door. He mustn't, he mustn't think about these things. Yes it might be her scarf but it might not. He couldn't very well take it home to find out, could he? This was all crazy; it could be anybody's scarf. Even if it were she might have just dropped by to say hello. But he couldn't take it home; he couldn't confront her with it. He wasn't that far gone, was he? He couldn't steal somebody's scarf just because he was a little bit crazy on the subject of his wife, could he? Hadn't he come there to try to get over this? Hadn't he come to ask Sammy to dinner for Christ's sake? Hadn't he?

Stuffed into the Envelope Between Ocean and Sky

Don't fall in love for a long enough time
and it gives you some perspective. You
remember rowing together out of sight of land,
you remember the haze, the glare, the light
turning white just above the surface
of the water. And the plentiful silence.
You remember looking away from her eyes,
which never left you, looking for dolphins,
sea gulls, flying fish. How empty everything
was! You remember the darkening of the sky,
the clouds, the distant sound of thunder. Don't
you remember? Summer storms sealed the horizon.

Winter Cruise

The horizon is never far enough away that
when the wind is blowing you can't see
the saw-tooth edge the waves make of it
against the sky. But today everything is serene.
You lie beside me asleep in your deck chair,
one finger folded into the middle of your book,
while on the immense ocean nothing stirs;
oh, a stray breeze here and there checks
the surface, but otherwise all is calm.
                                        Yet I
cannot forget the north. We are a thousand miles
free of it but I cannot let it be,
something in me conjures it up, the granite hills
heavy with snow, the cold, the aboriginal forests.
Here we are, at peace, and I can think only
of the gulls huddled against the northwest
gales, of the pitiless first crossings, lonely
little shiploads of desperate dreamers picking maggots
out of the flour, nothing ahead of them but winter.
Troubled, I gaze out toward the long flat margins
of the known world, a kind of uneasy wonder
filling me. How expensive everything is! To get
us here cost a history of suffering, whole ships
buried at sea, while even now a bitter cold sleet
somewhere costs somebody something.

                    And you asleep.
You will wake up soon and look toward the horizon
to see that nothing has changed, and nothing has.
Then you will look at me and smile, all afternoon
in it, all its stillness, all its warmth. And this
would be enough, in another mood. But the chill
that has gotten into me is too old, too real.
The ocean makes no promises. This peace
in a number of other directions turns to ice.

Summer of '69

We went to the beach and found
too many unexplained shells. The kids
built fortresses in the sand,
while older waves of boys rode
hard ashore. Were we at war?
We scanned the horizon repeatedly,
waiting for news. Gulls flew sortie
after sortie, and crabs dug in. There
was no shelter anywhere. Were we
at war? Nobody seemed to know. Bodies
were scattered all over the beach. The tide
relentlessly rose against us. The enemy
could have been anyone under the sun.
Were we at war? Guards spoke of the undertow,
dragging us farther out than we wanted to go.

Out Far and in Deep

for Peter Dee

It seemed so vast that day as to be abstract,
like femininity, perhaps, or even more like
Transcendentalism, which would have abolished
limits entirely and taken up so much room
in the pool of our understanding as to crowd us
out. But we went swimming anyway
in this our ocean, gauging her mood as men do,
always unprepared as men are for her shifts,
her—what shall I call them? —her waves of passion,
her emotional power. We had both mastered her
more than once, she that cannot be mastered,
and the brotherhood of our arrogance almost swept us
away. (But what was it Emerson said? He spoke
of a wild delight, and he said that Nature suffers
nothing to remain in her that cannot escape
on its own.)
                    Friend, it was dangerous
to swim. The Atlantic has a bottomless appetite
for men. The wind was blowing her hair
into our eyes. It was as if, having loved,
the two of us, the one woman, we had leapt
to the same shallow conclusion about them all.
It was as if we thought it would be enough
not to drown to put into a few spare words
about her our brusque, male, minimal sense of awe.

Putting Real Distance Between Us

Finding myself by the Atlantic at dawn
I quieted down enough to walk
a ways and remember how I got there
and even think a little about you.
Then suddenly there was the sun, the first
rays like fingers, as they say, feeling
me out.
            You must have done this
to me, too, before you left, held me
at arm's length like a satellite, like
a basketball player palming the ball.

Walls

There cannot be only the sky
and men. More must happen. Like a landscape
painting it must fill up, the Dutch
must come, bourgeois, rich, and love
things, the fish out of the sea, the great
profusion of their still lifes, then Impressionism
and its flowers. Lying on my back
on the beach I see this now. You
are not enough, even you leaning
over me, whispering something to me
about the sun. We need walls, and we need
to cover them with absorbing distractions.

The Seven Stages of Divorce and the Four Shorelines

But as in landlessness alone resides highest truth, shoreless, indefinite as God—so better is it to perish in that howling infinite, than be ingloriously dashed upon the lee, even if that were safety!

-Herman Melville, *Moby Dick*

The land may vary more;
But wherever the truth may be—
The water comes ashore,
And the people look at the sea.

-Robert Frost, "Neither Out Far Nor in Deep"

One: Sagg Main

Sagg Main is the name of the beach at the end of Sagg Road, which runs south through the center of Sagaponack, New York, a small hamlet in the Hamptons with a population composed in the winter mostly of potato and horse farmers, and in the summer a sprinkling of the rich and famous as well. It isn't hard to see what attracts the latter. Sagaponack is unusually pretty; there is a post office, a small store that feeds local people and the rich and famous indiscriminately, and a two-room schoolhouse that still functions. The hamlet has no real center. The land is flat and open and serene, the farms and farm houses are old and established, and everything seems spread out with an even hand between the highway and the sea. It seems peaceful, wearing the kind of peace that only age can grant. The graveyards are small, unpretentious, and full. The trees that line Sagg Road have been there a long time. Pheasants roam the fields.

As for the beach, it is as fine, if not as wide, as any beach in California. The parking lot at the beach holds perhaps 150 cars. Every summer weekend it fills up; people gather their beach chairs and their umbrellas and their children and drive to Sagg Main and do what people do at beaches. They line up close to the water, chairs facing it, and sit down and read, or talk, and sometimes swim. Sometimes they sleep. Sometimes they just sit and stare at the ocean. It is as Robert Frost's poem says: the people look at the sea. They turn their back on the land.

On many of those weekends, I am among these people. I come like everyone else with my beach chair and a book to read, my sun screen, my towel, and sit like everyone else close to the ocean, facing it. I have done this all my life, not necessarily at Sagg Main but elsewhere, in New Jersey, in California, on whatever coast I have happened to be. I have spent who knows how many months, indeed years, if you add the hours up, sitting on beaches facing the ocean, or walking up and down the beach beside it. I still don't quite know why. Maybe it's as Melville says: the truth is out there, shoreless and indefinite. These in any case are my texts, my anchors, if you will, Frost and Melville; they have come as close as anyone to this longing for the ocean, this need to be near it, to look at it, to look for something in it. For the truth, perhaps, howling and infinite. For the truth, perhaps, wherever and whatever it may be.

And yet I must offer at the very beginning this paradox, that the—what shall I call it?—the disturbance I want to talk about, the epicenter, you might call it, of my life, reached its climax not on a beach but in the mountains. In Rocky Mountain National Park, to be specific. I was there with my first wife and my son, who was twelve years old at the time. We were on a trail on Flattop Mountain, climbing toward the top. At about 10,000 feet they ran out of energy. I was acclimatized; I had been in Colorado for four or five days, I was used to the altitude. They had just arrived. So at 10,000 feet they told me that they simply could not go on. But I could. I wanted to go on. I was close enough to the top that I could see it, and I knew I would never come back, not to that particular place. I knew I had to go on. Wait for me, I said, and went on climbing.

It took a long time; and then, when I got to the top, I went into a kind of ecstasy at the view, which seemed to stretch in all directions for a hundred miles, and I stayed too long. When I came back down the trail they were not there, not at the place where I had left them. They had gone back down on their own. I thought I would probably catch up to them, but I didn't. I waded through the mud and the snow that was still on the trail in shady areas, I followed the trail into the tree line, I hurried with a growing sense of anxiety down the mountain. They were nowhere to be found. Finally I reached the parking lot and the car, but they weren't there, either. I was sure by now that something terrible had happened to them and that I had done the wrong thing to leave them unprotected high up on a mountain, a woman and a child in a strange place, a strange country. And then, ten minutes into panic, they showed up. They had lost their way on the mountain, lost the trail and had come to some dangerous scree and scrambled down, almost falling any number of times, said my wife. She was very angry. She said I had abandoned them. I should have stayed with them. A marten had frightened her. I shouldn't have kept on going. It was irresponsible of me, she said, and she was right.

Yet I wasn't sorry. I felt a little guilty, but I wasn't sorry. I said I was, but I wasn't. The mountain had meant too much to me. To be that close, and not go to the top: without question I was selfish about it, without question I was irresponsible. But I had to go on to the top. Or, if I did not have to, if it was not exactly something I was compelled to do, nevertheless I did. And that very night was the night I told my wife I was going to leave her. That was the night I told her I didn't want to be married to her any more. After eighteen years of marriage, I was through. Not because she got angry, not at all. It was simply over. I was not angry in return. It was simply over, and I was not sorry I had gone on.

Oddly enough I had dreamt this event years before, not with any exactitude, to be sure, but in substance. I had had a dream in which the four of us, husband, wife, daughter and son, were driving along and had come to a mountain and decided to climb it. My daughter, however, stayed in the car, and she did not, in fact, come to Colorado with us. So my son, my wife and I got out of the car, and we climbed up a trail, but at some point there was a gap in the mountain, a kind of hiatus that had to be struggled across, like a crevasse but horizontal, not vertical. I got across this gap, and so did my son, who went on ahead of me; but my wife could not make the leap. I tried to help her, but she could not do it. So I went on to the top and my son was already there, standing there with drums, playing them with extraordinary skill and abandon, as if he were celebrating some momentous occasion.

What I want to say is that life has a kind of starkness to it. Because in all this what I best remember is not anything I have described so far, but rather something utterly unrelated: the outline that another mountain made, a very close neighbor to the one I was climbing, against the absolutely cloudless Colorado sky. Against the purity of the blue, black stone and white snow. It was stunningly beautiful, and it is etched upon my mind. And what I did that night was also stark, and grotesque as well, and awful. Yet in a strange way beautiful. We have come to Colorado for a vacation, and I am telling you that I am about to leave you. Forever. Yet even while I recognize how terrible a thing this is to do and how culpable I am to do it, with no warning, with no hesitation, I am not sorry. I was sad. I cried a great deal, and so did she. But I was not sorry. I am still not sorry. I make no apologies whatsoever. The cut was lovely; it was clean.

Oddest of all, perhaps, is the fact that I love the mountains much more than I love the beach, yet I am seldom in the mountains. In truth it would be wrong to say that I love the beach at all.

Mountains fill me with excitement; they move me; I am driven to climb them. Yet I am seldom there, not once in five years. But I live seven miles from the beach at Sagg Main. I can be there in ten minutes. But I do not love it. Perhaps it is too familiar to me, or it is too hot in summer, too cold in winter. I don't know. Yet it is near a beach that I have chosen to live. Go figure.

Two: Long Beach Island

I was born too late to see it but Long Beach Island had a railroad that came on at Surf City, about halfway down the length of the island, and then ran south to Beach Haven. Long Beach Island is exactly what its name implies, a long beach, eighteen miles from tip to tip, and about a quarter of a mile wide. It's a barrier beach, a sandbar, really, nothing more. The idea of a railroad on it always struck me as incongruous. From an early age the island seemed fragile to me, while trains were massive, heavy affairs. The island is indeed fragile. In 1962 a winter storm cut it in pieces. Old beach houses that had somehow survived for two or three generations were washed away. It was a sad thing, but predictable. In 1944 a hurricane struck the island; I was seven years old at the time. We drove down afterwards to see if our house was still there. It was, but in our front yard sat a thirty-five foot powerboat. Houses on the ocean at the head of our street had had the sand underneath them half washed away; they sat there precariously, tilting toward the surf, ready at any moment to collapse. This was a powerful lesson at seven years of age. The ocean bears things away. The works of man do not endure; if they do, it is at the whim of natural forces.

Some part of me, I must confess, exulted at this news, even at seven. My brother and I listened enviously to the stories of a young friend whose family had ridden out the storm on the island. He talked most vividly, I remember, about watermelons floating down the street on the seawater that was overflowing the dunes and invading the island. They belonged to a neighbor, and he rushed out into the howling wind to grab one. He was himself only eleven or twelve years old, my brother's age. Many years later, when I was myself married and taking my own family, my wife, my two children, to the island every summer, I came across a story in a local paper about a ship that had been wrecked in a much earlier storm, a spring storm in April of 1854. I was so struck by the story that I still have it. The ship was the Powhatan, a clipper ship bound for New York with a crew of 29 and 311 passengers, all of them German immigrants wanting to start a new life here in the United States. It was a Sunday. The storm was a snowstorm, blinding and cold, and the Powhatan ran aground off Surf City shortly after dawn. The nearest rescue equipment was five miles away. Men struggled to drag it through the sand, into the wind and snow, to the site of the wreck, but they could not do it; they returned to shelter lest they perish themselves. A few watched helplessly on the beach while the ship slowly turned its side on to the waves. Every wave swept a few passengers off, and this went on all day long. Some climbed into the rigging, but the wind and the cold numbed their hands and fingers; they could not hold on; they dropped into the sea. At five in the afternoon a huge wave swept the remaining passengers and crew off the boat. Every single person on board died. That night another boat grounded near the wreck of the Powhatan. This time one man survived.

I read the story and I knew when I read it that I would have to retell it eventually, I would have to put it down on paper and try to explain why it gave me such fierce pleasure. But I cannot explain it. I am not a bad man. I do not whoop over the Holocaust; when people die in an earthquake I do not applaud. But there is something hard and cruel in me that nothing reaches. That refuses all touch. I am half afraid that it might be my soul.

A railroad, then: the idea interested me, even at an early age. How temporary things are! Even islands can disappear, especially islands. When I drove the family down every summer I can remember fantasizing, as we crossed the big bridge that spans the inland waterway, the channel that runs behind Long Beach Island, driving straight onto the beach. You can see the beach and the ocean from this bridge, which is of course perpendicular to the island itself, and I would imagine that instead of turning south toward our house two miles down we would just keep on driving straight, onto the beach, into the surf. I don't think this is an uncommon fantasy. We see pickup trucks on the beach at Sagg Main all the time in the spring and fall; young men drive on with their gear and their dogs and go fishing. On television, car ads sometimes show cars driving on the hard sand next to the surf, splashing water into a graceful curve.

I never did, in fact, drive onto the beach. The car would have gotten stuck in the sand. It would have seemed extremely foolish to me, like the railroad. No, I drove south to the house, my parents' little house that we borrowed for two or three weeks every summer, and we all went faithfully to the beach, which my wife loved, and my children, too, and I came to hate it over the years, the routine, two hours in the morning, two hours in the afternoon, lying there on the sand absorbing the sunlight, reading, perhaps, taking walks, watching the children play. An island. There was no place to go. I couldn't get away from them. Everything was too close. The beach was too crowded. Underneath ran the unspoken assumption that we were very much at peace, and that we all loved each other. It wasn't true. I took to going to the beach late, after the lifeguard had gone, and swimming out by myself as far as I liked. During the day I stayed home and read Dickens. Novel after novel. At five I went to the beach. The little family groups had all gone home by then, the sun was less intense, and I swam. I swam far out, all by myself, to the limits of my own safety, my ability to make it back. It was always a moment of fierce pleasure. It felt almost like some sort of redemption.

Three: Big Sur

I spent the summer of 1973 on a research trip across the United States; the research was for a book on the mentally ill and the trip culminated in California. In Big Sur. Once I found Big Sur, it was hard to go anywhere else. I had fitted an old van out with a mattress in the back to keep my costs down and I used to sleep in the van parked in the parking lot at Pfeiffer Beach State Park. It was against the law, but the rangers only hassled you once in a while. Lots of other people were sleeping there, too, most of them hippies of one kind or another. But it was 1973, and by this time hippies had an edge to them. In the midst of my sojourn I spent two days in Los Angeles, then on my way back picked up some hippies hitchhiking out of Santa Barbara. It was their habit then to hang out on the highway where it ran through the center of Santa Barbara and you had to slow down. I picked up four of them, two men, two women. One of the men was a Vietnam veteran. He carried a huge knife. I dropped all four of them at Pfeiffer Beach; when I left, they had surrounded a wild boar that had wandered down out of the hills. It was crazy. Wild boars are dangerous. You don't surround a wild animal. I told them what they were doing was stupid, but they didn't care. The Vietnam vet was by this time threatening to kill any ranger who tried to drive him off the beach. He seemed crazy enough to do just that.

I made the trip alone. Before I left I had told my wife I didn't know if I wanted to stay married any longer. I spent a week in Kansas, picked up a hitchhiker in Wyoming. We drove across the rest of the West together. In Lovelock, Nevada, —yes, Lovelock; that was the name—where we stopped for lunch, I called home and told her that I had been thinking about it and had decided that I did want to stay married, or thought I did. She didn't say much. What was there to say? It all seemed to be in my hands. Passively, quietly, she was waiting it out. That fact alone should have been a sign that it was only a matter of time. A woman who wants to keep you doesn't sit quietly at home and wait it out. Isn't that the case? If there's anguish, if there's passion, doesn't it have to emerge?

Maybe not. I don't know. I got to Big Sur and hung out with the hippies. One of them was a girl I'll call Sylvia. She wore a strapless green dress with an elastic top, like a tank top, that cinched around the breasts. I think it was her only outfit. She came across me at the beach and the first thing she said to me was, "I bet you a pack of cigarettes you can't guess the size of my areola."

"Look," I replied, "if you want a pack of cigarettes I'll just buy you one. Come on."

We got in the van and I drove her to the nearest store and on the way I did guess the size of her areola, and she showed me her breasts and of course I had guessed wrong. Then we drove up Partington Ridge Road, where Henry Miller had lived, and on the way I parked the van in a little pull-off in the trees; she was in the back, stretched out on the mattress, taking a nap. I joined her there. She had pulled her dress down to her waist. It was only a few minutes before I was making love to her. "You've got the hands of a drummer, " she told me. She told me exactly what to do. When we were done we climbed back into the front seats and drove the rest of the way, to a house that was occupied by people from the Arica Institute, one of the enlightenment shops of the time. We drove into the yard, and there were four totally naked men, two of them with guitars, one with drums, and the fourth with a saxophone, playing music that was not rock, not jazz, but something in between: jamming, in any case. A fifth man was watering some plants. On a table facing the musicians a beautiful young woman, naked like the rest, was standing on one leg in a yoga position. Sylvia got out of the van and started to dance. Me? I got out of the van and stared at the Pacific. We were 2,000 feet above sea level and the afternoon sun was turning the surface of the ocean into silver. Below us the Santa Lucia range dropped down in a kind of cascade of landscape. On the steep hillsides the grass had turned yellow and brown while the redwoods kept the sharp declivities green. I had never seen it all from this height and it was staggering. The coast was visible for thirty or forty miles in each direction. Mountain succeeded upon mountain into the distance. And to the west the vast Pacific, the unimaginable expanse of it, lay calm and shining at the foot of my gaze.

Sylvia and I spent 24 hours together before I tired of her and dropped her off where I had found her. She took me to a party that night and we got stoned and retired to somebody's bedroom and went at it again, and somebody walked in on us, a whole crew walked in on us, but nobody seemed to care. I certainly didn't care. We slept that night at Pfeiffer Beach; she had brought somebody else along, a young man with a backpack, and she wanted all three of us to sleep together in the back of the van but there wasn't enough room and I wasn't going to do that anyway. Sylvia would have slept with the Mexican army: you got that feeling. She told me she had slept with sixty men in as many days. She told me she thought I was her Saint Luke. A healer, she explained. She told me her parents had kicked her out of the house permanently when they caught her screwing her boyfriend in the bushes just under the bay window. Let's stick to the facts. I didn't tire of her. She scared me. She fascinated me, too. She was on far more of a trip, if you'll pardon the expression, than I was. She scared the hell out of me.

So I dumped her, and then I tried to find her again. She had disappeared. I felt guilty; I felt excited; I felt stupid. But I knew I was out of my depth. Hook up with Sylvia and God knows what would happen. It took me only one more day to call my wife and ask her to bring the children out and we would all go home together. We would drive north, up the coast, I said, and then cut east after we reached Washington. We would see Mt. Rainier, I said. We would see Yellowstone. I went to the Phoenix, which is a shop in Big Sur housed in the building that was once the home of Rita Hayworth and Orson Welles, and I bought them all gifts. In the four days before they arrived I turned another girl down flat. Enough was enough. I wanted to stay married, didn't I?

It is not easy to tell the truth about all this because it looks so bad. But all this is in fact the truth. And if you want things to be worse they were worse. I never felt guilty about Sylvia. A certain amount of shame, yes, but shame and guilt are not identical; shame is when other people find out and you feel abashed because you have violated the proprieties; when you are driving, alone in the car, and you stop for a light and you notice that somebody in the next car has seen you picking your nose, that's shame. My wife did find out about Sylvia. I had to tell her because Sylvia gave me a disease. I had to tell my wife because I didn't want to pass it on. But I felt no guilt when I told her. I had betrayed her, but the feelings that ought to have accompanied betrayal did not come. I was much more embarrassed than guilty. I was not sorry. I had done what I had done, without appreciable regret. I was not sorry.

The capacity for being sorry had already vanished from the relationship. It was all only a matter of time.

Nor should anyone think for a moment that this account is confessional and that by confessing I hope to be redeemed. I am not so cowardly as that. On the contrary, I tell these stories with a certain pride. I have believed since my divorce that you know nothing of yourself until you have done serious damage to another person; and if it was my wife I damaged, at least I kept it within the family.

Four: San Pedro

For Frost and for Melville both the ocean stands halfway between metaphor and reality, and that is what I am after; that's where the truth lies, in between. I took a ferry once from Orient Point on Long Island to New London in Connecticut; it was in January, it was threatening snow, and I remember looking down at the water, watching it, as the ferry pulled into the harbor in New London, and seeing the kinds of constantly shifting patterns the motion of the water made, the dark green of the water and the flat aluminum of the reflected sky moving in constantly shifting planes. These planes were opaque. This was not water you could see into. A few days later I was in the Museum of Modern Art in New York and found myself in front of Jackson Pollock's painting *Full Fathom Five*, and there it was, that same impenetrable surface, those same shifting planes of dark green and aluminum promising a depth they do not deliver. He had seen it, too. Truth is liquid, a friend of mine once said. I would add that it lies somewhere between metaphor and reality.

San Pedro is in Belize, on a peninsula that stretches down from Mexico just to the north, and I did not visit it until six or seven years after it was over, after the divorce, after I had remarried. It was my second wife and I who made this trip. But we are talking about the stages of divorce, which occur when they occur. And in San Pedro we dove; Belize has the longest unbroken reef line in the Western Hemisphere, in San Pedro it is only a few hundred yards off shore, and we dove it five times. Never having done this before, we put on scuba gear and rode out to the reef in a motorboat at breakneck speed with our divemaster, who was a Mayan Indian covered with tatoos named Adolpho Ayuso, and dove to progressively greater depths on each dive, until, the last two times, we reached 85 feet, where the reef ends and it plunges straight down into the abyss. We learned, so to speak, as we went.

It is the abyss that I remember most vividly. Oh, the reef itself, yes! What a profusion of life! Yellowtail snappers and sergeant majors in huge schools, all turning and wheeling at once, goatfish, spotted drums, butterfly fish, jacks and tangs, grunts, the blue chromis, the yellowtail damselfish, flounder, moray eels, eagle rays, little highhats, durgons, filefish and queen triggerfish, nurse sharks, barracudas, parrotfish and hogfish, all kinds of wrasses, soldierfish, angelfish, blue hamlets, groupers, the harlequin bass: these are only the fish. Corals of all kinds, sea fans, sea turtles, anemones, plume worms, sponges. Every square inch of surface, every cubic foot of water, had something in it that was alive. Fish drifted through our arms inches from our faces. After the first dive we could not get enough. Coming down the anchor line toward the reef we felt like new souls must feel drifting down from the empty blue heavens toward life.

Then you turn away. You look over the edge of the reef, you look at what they call the wall, and it is indeed like a wall, it plunges straight down, and you can't see anything but the water darkening at some indeterminate distance below you and the wall disappearing into that distance. Someone has already told you that it is some thousands of feet to the bottom. This wall is a sheer cliff thousands of feet high. And when you look not down but out, towards the Caribbean, you see nothing but blue water: no life, no profusion, only the blue of the water stretching you do not know how many thousands of miles east, to the islands, to Africa, whatever is out there. You draw back. Looking away from the reef turns out to be insupportable. The word "abyss" acquires an unexpected resonance; it reacquires some of its Miltonic power. You look anxiously around for the others, for your wife, for Adolpho. You keep an eye on your wife, to make sure she doesn't wander inadvertently into that vastness. You see once again what life is, a project, an enterprise, edging into the waste spaces, but not necessarily successfully. And a kind of terror can grip you. You have to fight it off. You are 85 feet beneath the surface of the ocean, 85 feet from the air you have to breathe to live. I will not say that terror gripped me. But it was close by.

Don't ask me when, we are talking about stages, not chronologies, but we used to hike in the Shawangunks, my first wife and I. The 'Gunks, as climbers call them, are actually a long ridge line east of the Catskills in New York noted for a rock-climbing area, a sheer rock wall perhaps 400 or 500 feet high running northeast for a mile or two near New Paltz. For climbers, it's one of the best areas in the East; but you don't have to be a climber to hike there. Trails run from a couple of roads right along the top of the cliffs, and we used to hike there once in a while. On one of these hikes—it must have been in the early '70s—we found an overlook where you could stand at the edge of the cliff and look out and down, straight down, to the woods and the rocks 400 feet below. My wife stood directly in front of me at this overlook, and right at the edge. No one else was around.

I had to grab a sapling with both hands to keep from pushing her to her death.

Which is a way of saying that one of the stages of divorce, if it is really meant, really felt, is always murder.

But it goes beyond that. It goes beyond the observation that the abysses are inside us as well as out, which is too easy, too obvious. The fact is, I truly loved my wife. I cared about what happened to her. Twenty minutes later, in a grove of trees, I made love to her, I remember. It took her by surprise, and me, too. When the divorce came I gave her everything, the house, the car, the savings account. The children. It wasn't enough, it turned out, but the love was there. The hatred. The indifference. Dozens of other feelings. All of it mixed up together, chaotic, feelings contradicting each other, confusing me, driving me into uncertainty and distraction.

Let me put it this way, but only with the understanding that I am speaking metaphorically: at the edge, at the juncture of profusion and emptiness, life and void, love and murder, truth is liquid. It cannot be held very long in anyone's hands. And this is a fact that has its counterpart in the real world. Some of the most fearsome creatures on the reef, for example, were the easiest to approach. Once Adolpho dove below us and grabbed an eagle ray, a strange fish shaped like a delta wing bomber with a wingspan of up to eight feet, by his long and dangerous spine of a tail and gave it a shake. He swam away. Adolpho showed us moray eels in their holes in the coral, their heads sticking out, and went up and patted them on the head. He found a nurse shark slumbering quietly, his eyes open, under a shelf of coral. We swam to within five feet of it and paused and looked. Murder is never the whole story. I have spent my whole life passing up opportunities to kill the ones I loved.

Five: Big Sur

In the end I wanted to kill both of us. We took a vacation in February of 1975. We flew to California, rented a car, spent a day or two in Los Angeles and then drove north up the coast toward Big Sur, where the hedge roses were in bloom. On the whole it was a lovely time. We spent most of a day on Pfeiffer Beach, which is a strip of sand perhaps a mile long closed at both ends by tall hills that plunge straight into the ocean. At low tide we walked around the headland to the north, saw sea otters playing in the surf among the rocks, and found another beach, untouched, no footprints upon it, no access to it. We walked in the redwood grove at the Big Sur Inn, climbed a hill near Pfeiffer Beach and from that vantage point saw a school of dolphins swimming south. We climbed Mt. Manuel one day and watched the hawks soaring and brought back a huge pine cone from the top, a pine cone a foot long. Another day we were sitting at a picnic table outside a little store on the coast road and looked up across the road to the hill opposite and saw a mountain lion on the side of the hill, moving across a clearing.

I think we both believed that this was a wonderful vacation, and that we were happy. But our last day there we were driving south along the coast highway back toward Big Sur from Carmel and Monterey through patches of fog. The highway curls around the sides of the mountains; it is an engineering marvel, all sharp curves over precipitous drops, a terrifying and exhilarating drive. Suddenly I felt an indescribable longing. When we reached the curves and I had to follow them, I did not want to. I wanted to go straight, over the edge of the road, down to the rocks hundreds of feet below. This longing was so powerful and so unexpected that I had to grip the wheel and consciously force myself to keep the car on the road; I had to think as I came to every curve, and there were scores of them, now it is time to turn right, now left, control yourself, you are in control, stay in control. I fell silent, unable to respond to my wife's anxious inquiries as to what was wrong. I gripped the wheel in a kind of fury. Later I was unable to explain to her what had happened. I could not explain it to myself. In the midst of all that scenery, all that prettiness, something had welled up inside and gripped my heart that would have driven us both over the edge to certain death.

Six: Long Beach Island

Was it the tedium, the sameness? Divorce is so difficult to explain. I never caught her with another man. She never spent money extravagantly. She felt no need to go off and find herself. She didn't lose her looks. She spent the best part of her life trying to be a good woman, and a good wife.

It was always I who was chipping away at this marriage, I who cheated, who had to go off by myself, who made friends who could not be her friends. What was it that kept getting into me? We know so little about love and what it does to people and how often it leads to violence.

I remember taking her out in a sailboat one of the first times we went to Long Beach Island. She got seasick. She got seasick on any boat. I grew up owning and racing small sailboats; they were important to me. Sailing is one of the few things you can do that is lyrical by its very nature. I sailed in the bay waters between Long Beach Island and the mainland, the waters of Barnegat Bay and Little Egg Harbor, among the marsh islands; I explored the mainland creeks, often alone, 12, 13, 14 years old, sailed up and down the inland waterway. I was an awkward, lonely, pimply boy who felt inadequate everywhere but on a boat. Of the four elements water was definitely mine. Once when I was 12 I tried to sail my sneakbox through the winding channel that ran between the two halves of a marsh called Flat Island. It was perhaps 150 yards from one end of the channel to the other, and I got a third of the way into it before I ran aground. It was low tide. In another hour or two, if I sat there and waited, I would have floated free, but I didn't have the patience to do that; besides, there was nothing to protect me from the sun. Those marshes have nothing on them but marsh grass, and they're full of greenhead flies. I had sailed through there before, but never at this low a tide. So there was nothing to do but to get out of the boat and pull it through the channel to the end. But I had not counted on the bay muck. Elsewhere you could walk on it; the water was generally deep enough that it took most of your weight, and the muck underneath would support you. But not where you're in less than a foot of water. Even at 12, I was heavy enough that at every step I took my leg sank into the muck most of its length, well past my knee. And the muck was full of the old shells of razor clams. When I came out of the channel at the other end and climbed back into the boat my legs were covered with long bloody scratches that ran, some of them, from my ankles almost up to my crotch. But I felt no chagrin. I felt, on the contrary, rather proud. I had waded through an ordeal.

I tell this story because even at 12 you can come to understand things about life; you can come to understand that if you have to do something and you know that it is going to cause you pain, the doing of it can become a kind of tonic. It can give you pleasure, put you on a kind of high. And perhaps this explains, in a sense, the divorce: knowing the pain it was going to cause on all sides, the enormous pain that would, indeed, never quite go away, nevertheless plunging ahead with it gave me a pleasure at least equal to the pain. At least I would no longer be stuck in the mud, if you will. Not that this metaphor is any more precise than the others. But I had to get out, clearly. The sun, the flies. . . .

She could not go sailing so she went to the beach. She loved the beach unequivocally. She had olive skin and seldom burned; she only got darker. After hours in the sun, she glowed with health. It was one of the small things I hated her for. I hated her for her goodness as well, the unambiguous face she presented to the world. I hated her selflessness. I hated the fact that it would never have occurred to her to murder me. I hated having nothing to fear from her, and therefore nothing to learn.

Of course I loved her too. Haven't I said that? Hadn't we been married for eighteen years, and happily for much of that time? I have photographs of us all on the beach in our bathing suits, husband and wife and two children, playing games with a ball or building sand castles or splashing about in the waves, smiling, laughing; and it was the same beach my parents had brought me to when I was a little boy, the same beach I had known all my life, the same long barrier beach stretched like a dike down the length of the New Jersey coast, protecting the flat marshes and the mainland behind from the violence and power and unpredictability of the Atlantic. Shielding the mainland from harm, as it were. I loved her, and my life was one long cord firmly attached to this island, and I had brought her here and she loved it, too, loved the beach, the sun, the waves. What happened to us? Everything ought to have been so simple; we ought to have just gone on.

Seven: Sagg Main

She came here once to visit my daughter, who was spending the summer working in a local restaurant and living in a rental on the other side of town. They went to the beach at Sagg Main, the two of them, and a friend of mine saw them there and was surprised, he told me later, because she didn't look like someone I would have been married to.

The divorce was bitter, bitter and ruinous, but the bitterness was not mine. I had left her well before I left her. We parted, incidentally, on July 4, 1976, the 200th anniversary of the signing of the Declaration of Independence. My life is full of this metaphorical resonance, but I have never known if the metaphors are real.

We spent the first four days of our honeymoon on Nantucket. She got seasick on the ferry going over. We were supposed to spend a week, but after four days I couldn't stand it and we went back to Cape Cod and joined another couple who had been married the same day we were. I was already unhappily married.

We talk about the truth, and this is a true story. But it only looks one way; it is my story, my version of events, partial by definition and deeply self-involved. She lives in the Southwest now, in mountainous country, a long way from any coastline. That, too, could be a fact that resonates. Melville thought that the ocean was a metaphor for the truth, the ocean in storm, howling and infinite, and it is a powerful metaphor. But the pure, thin air at high altitudes, and the distances you can see: what is this if not another entrance to eternity?

It is so tempting, always, to stretch metaphor too far. "Wherever the truth may be—," said Frost, "The water comes ashore, / And the people look at the sea." We live out our metaphors. We adopt them and live them out. Thus marriage is a metaphor for love. What is divorce, then? We know so little; we live through our metaphors, they constitute our experience, but mostly it is a matter of waiting. We wait for things to come clear. We wait for someone to explain it all to us, for the metaphor to develop its meaning. In the end, I have come to think, that's what the people along the sand may be doing; Frost was right about it, perhaps, they are keeping watch, they are waiting. We talk about the truth and we wait for it on the beach because we have this sense, this suspicion, that truth emerges, that it rises up out of the depths of our experience into the light, that it gathers strength and appears out of the flux, the constant movement and change that life is.

Is this true?

I don't know. It's so hard to pin down the reasons for what people do.

I don't know, for example, whether if I hadn't left her I would have been able to stay. If I had chosen to stay, that is, would I have been able to? And what would that have done to me? I don't know.

I don't know if her pain, which was clearly massive, was worth my freedom.

For that matter I don't know if leaving her made me free.

I could go on with these questions, but what would be the point? As I write it is summer and people are returning to the beaches. Every weekend now the Sagg Main parking lot fills up. I go sometimes and line up along the sand with the rest. For the most part I am content with things, I am even serene. I have my questions and they remain with me, but they do not torment me, and I have no solid hope of an answer in any case. Truth is liquid, my friend told me, and I have no reason to think he is wrong. Nevertheless I sit there gazing out to sea like the rest, living the metaphor out. Like them I am keeping watch, I am waiting, and I know what I am waiting for.

I am waiting for something to emerge. Keats has a line that expresses it well. I am waiting, as he put it, for the whale's back in the sea of prose.

Cover painting by Sallie Quirk

Cover design by Gerald Pryor

Design and typesetting by Stefanie Kott,
DesKott Publishing, Fort Lee, NJ,
and Southampton, NY

Printed by The Studley Press,
Dalton, Massachusetts